Out to Lunch

WITH

Brian Turner

Recipes from the 1999 Series

Including About Anglia 'Quick Cooking' Recipes
from Brian Turner

ANGLIA
Television Limited

This book contains recipes from the
Anglia Television series Out to Lunch
with Brian Turner (shown Spring and
Autumn 1999) and About Anglia
'Quick Cooking' strand (shown
spring 1999).

Published in 1999 by Anglia Television
Ltd, Anglia House, Norwich NR1 3JG,
United Kingdom

www.angliatv.co.uk

ISBN 0 906836 37 9

un A United News & Media company

Many other traditional recipes – and
variations on some of those featured in
this series of OUT TO LUNCH – can
be found in several books researched
and written by well-known Norfolk
cookery writer Mary Norwak.

These include:

Cakes, A Book of Best British Recipes
(Batsford 1984);

A Taste of Norfolk (Jarrolds 1989 – to
mark British Food and Farming Year);

English Puddings, Sweet and Savoury
(Batsford 1981 hardback, Sphere 1984
paperback).

Book production
Editors: Colin Bevan and Robin Bray
Researcher: David Leverett
Production assistant: Tina Ball
Designer: Colin Edwards
Printer: Reflex Litho, Thetford
Photographs © Anglia Television Ltd

Programme production
Out to Lunch
Series producer/director: Paul Freeman
Food stylist/home economist: Anne Stirk
Researcher: June Collen

About Anglia 'Quick Cooking'
Series producer: Eddie Anderson
Quick Cooking producer: Paul Freeman
Food stylist/home economist: Anne Stirk

Suppliers credits
Ashmore for Trugs; Boots PLC;
Chasseur cast iron pans/casseroles;
Dudson crockery; Henckels knives;
Lakeland Ltd; Le Creuset
pans/casseroles; Marks & Spencer
Home Stores; Mary Reader, Good
Grips Utensils and Denby Pottery;
Meyer for pans; Progress Bakeware;
Saffron PR Co.

CONTENTS

Recipes may vary in minor detail from those shown on screen.
In case of discrepancies those in this book should be followed.

TV CHEF BRIAN TURNER relished the chance to serve up a solid slice of time-honoured tradition in this third run of OUT TO LUNCH programmes.

For the series puts the emphasis on the long-established customs and seasoned ingredients of the East of England along with the people and recipes concerned with them.

Brian found out what put the 'Saffron' in front of 'Walden', went wildfowling in the Fens and traced the history of cider-making in Suffolk and mustard-making in Norwich.

He also sought out such specialists as traditional apple-growers, bakers, brewers, butchers, cheese-makers, meat and fish smokers and wine makers.

Then he used the wide range of produce from all these sources to cook up a tempting array of traditional dishes.

Within the following pages you'll find lambs' kidneys turbigo, rabbit saddle and welsh rarebit for starters, with beef wellington, belly of pork, devilled herrings, rack of lamb, steak and kidney pie and stuffed goose to follow.

Finally there's a collection of cakes, tarts and puddings to ensure that anyone with a sweet tooth is totally spoilt for choice!

As a bonus – for those who don't have much time to simmer and stir – there's also a selection of 'Quick Cooking' recipes demonstrated in ABOUT ANGLIA by Brian.

Even he found some of the offerings in the sweet section of the OUT TO LUNCH recipes particularly hard to resist: "I'm very keen on old-fashioned English puddings – and we had some real crackers," he enthused.

"The treacle tart in the first programme was great and my favourite was the bread and butter pudding with lashings of custard and cream."

Brian fosters a belief that traditional regional food has been making a deserved comeback after being somewhat out of fashion in the trendy Eighties.

"It uses fresh local products and is what I call real comfort food," he says. "It gives people a feel-good factor – and the message is that you don't have to be inventive or clever to enjoy good food!"

After three years of 'lunching out' in the East of England, Brian has fallen in love with it and has decided he wants to buy a home in the region.

"One day I'd like a little cottage in a small village – probably near the sea. I'd love to become one of the locals," he declares.

Ingredients

(Serves 12 – suitable for party – but quantity can be varied for 2, 4 or 6)

For the gravadlax:

4.5kg (10lb) salmon, filleted

4 tbsp sea salt

4 tbsp caster sugar

1 large bunch of dill

1 tbsp cognac

pepper

For the potato salad:

450g (1lb) small new potatoes

2 tbsp tinned consommé

3 tbsp mayonnaise

1 tbsp grain mustard

1 tbsp finely chopped onion or shallot

2 tbsp chopped chives

seasoning

1 tbsp vinaigrette dressing

Gravadlax Method

Make gravadlax 24 hours before using.

Scale fish and remove pin bones – or ask fishmonger to do this for you.

Mix together salt, sugar, dill, cognac and pepper.

Lay one piece of salmon, skin side down, on piece of aluminium foil.

Spread dill mixture over salmon.

Lay second piece of salmon on top, skin side up.

Fold over aluminium foil, seal edges well and place in fridge.

Leave fish to marinate for 24 hours, turning frequently.

Unwrap and pour away juices.

Cut into butterfly steaks and pan fry or griddle for 2-3 minutes each side.

Potato Salad Method

Wash potatoes. Cook in boiling water until soft and drain.

Heat consommé in a small pan.

Slice potatoes into consommé. Stir in mayonnaise and mustard.

Add onion, chives and seasoning.

To serve, pile potato salad in centre of dish or plate for individual serving.

Lay salmon on top and drizzle with vinaigrette.

NB Potato salad quantity given above serves FOUR but can be varied according to number of servings required.

LAMBS' KIDNEYS TURBIGO

Ingredients

(Serves 6 as starter)

12-18 'pickling' onions

10 lambs' kidneys, trimmed and halved

50g (2oz) butter

225g (8oz) chipolata sausages

225g (8oz) button mushrooms

1-2 tsp English mustard

2 tbsp sherry/port

150ml ($\frac{1}{4}$ pint) beef stock

salt and pepper

bay leaf

2-3 slices bread for croutes

Method

Blanch onions in boiling water for 3-4 minutes, alternatively cook in little stock from measured 150ml ($\frac{1}{4}$ pint). Drain.

Cut kidneys in half lengthways.

Heat sauté or deep frying pan, drop in butter and sauté kidneys until nicely browned. Lift out and keep warm.

Add chipolatas to pan, brown on all sides for 2 minutes, lift out and keep warm.

Add onions and mushrooms to pan and shake over brisk heat for 3-4 minutes.

Stir in mustard, sherry and stock, bring to boil and season.

Return sausages and kidneys to pan, along with bay leaf.

Cover and simmer for 20-25 minutes.

Meanwhile prepare the croutes.

Cut bread into heart shapes or triangles and fry gently in little hot oil until lightly golden brown.

Serve kidneys in dish, surrounded by croutes.

For special effect dip croutes in little chopped parsley.

RABBIT SADDLE

Ingredients
(Serves 6 as starter)

4 rabbit shoulders

2 cloves garlic, chopped

2 bay leaves

2 chicken legs, uncooked

salt and pepper

300ml ($\frac{1}{2}$ pint) double cream

1 tbsp tarragon

1 rabbit saddle

mixed salad leaves

For the dressing:

1 tbsp truffle oil

3 tbsp olive oil

1 tbsp white wine vinegar

1 tsp Dijon mustard

Method

Cook rabbit shoulders slowly in oil, using garlic and bay leaf to flavour.

When cooked, cool and shred.

Using chicken legs, make mousse in processor with salt and double cream.

Add rabbit and chopped tarragon. Mix together.

Bone out rabbit saddle from inside, leaving outside skin on.

Lay rabbit down, meat side up and season. Pile mousse on top.

Fold stomach flaps over and form enclosed sausage shape.

Roll up tightly in cling-film, then aluminium foil and steam for 12-15 minutes.

Allow to cool in foil.

Slice and serve on bed of leaves with truffle dressing, made by whisking together all ingredients.

Ingredients

(Serves 4)

For the welsh rarebit:

300ml (½ pint) double cream

4 tbsp beer

3-4 drops Worcestershire sauce

1 tsp English mustard

110g (4oz) well-flavoured local cheese, diced

2 egg yolks

4 slices thick bread, toasted

4 poached eggs

seasoning

For the vegetables:

olive oil

4 baby aubergines – or large aubergine, cut into slices

2 courgettes, thickly sliced

2 peppers, de-seeded and quartered

2 red onions, peeled – root core left intact – then quartered vertically

seasoning

For the dressing:

150ml (½ pint) olive oil

1 tsp English mustard

2 tbsp white wine vinegar

mixed leaves – rocket and spinach

Method

Place cream in pan and reduce by third.

Add beer and Worcestershire sauce.

Stir in mustard and cheese and allow mixture to melt and bubble.

Stir in egg yolks.

Spoon mixture onto toast.

Place under hot grill and cook until lightly browned and set.

Meanwhile, heat griddle pan and cook vegetables until charred slightly.

Drizzle with olive oil and season.

Mix up dressing and toss griddled vegetables in half. Keep warm.

Toss salad leaves in remainder of dressing.

To Assemble

Place salad on plate.

Arrange griddled vegetables around salad.

Top salad with rarebit and then poached egg.

Drizzle eggs with any remaining dressing.

Ingredients

(Serves 4)

25g (1oz) unsalted butter, for greasing

4 pieces fresh salmon, brill or plaice

300ml ($\frac{1}{2}$ pint) fish stock

1.25 litres (2 pints) fresh mussels

1 onion, chopped

1 leek, chopped

1 bulb of fennel, chopped

2 cloves garlic, chopped

parsley stalks – tied with string

1 glass white wine

150ml ($\frac{1}{4}$ pint) double cream

saffron stems, infused in a little white wine

50g (2oz) unsalted butter

16 new potatoes, cooked

6 plum tomatoes, peeled, de-seeded and diced

2 tbsp chopped chives

Method

Lay pieces of fish in buttered dish and season. Pour over the 300ml ($\frac{1}{2}$ pint) of fish stock and cover with buttered grease-proof paper.

Bake in oven for 5-10 minutes at 180°C/350°F/gas mark 4.

Remove and keep warm.

Reserve remaining cooking liquor.

Clean mussels. Place in large pan with chopped onion, leeks and fennel.

Add chopped garlic, parsley stalks and glass of wine. Cover, bring to boil and cook until mussels open.

Remove all mussels from pan, take half from shells and reserve remainder.

Place shelled mussels back in pan and add reserved fish cooking liquor. Reduce by approximately half.

Remove parsley stalks and process remaining mixture until smooth. Strain and place back in pan.

Add cream and reduce to consistency of single cream.

Add saffron liquor and stir in butter.

Reheat pre-cooked new potatoes.

Arrange fish in 4 bowls. Lay reserved mussels on top and place potatoes around fish.

Check seasoning in sauce and pour over fish.

Sprinkle with diced tomatoes and chopped chives and serve.

MAIN COURSES

DEVILLED HERRINGS *With Mustard Seed Sauce and Stir-Fried Cabbage*

Ingredients
(Serves 4)

For the herrings:

2 tbsp cayenne pepper

4 tbsp plain flour

8 herrings, filleted

50g (2oz) butter

For the mustard seed sauce:

2 shallots, finely chopped

½ leek, chopped

bay leaf

50g (2oz) unsalted butter

300ml (½ pint) dry white wine

600ml (1 pint) fish stock

300ml (½ pint) double cream

2-3 tsp grainy mustard

For the cabbage:

50g (2oz) butter

garlic clove, crushed

225g (8oz) cabbage, white or green

seasoning

Method

First prepare herrings.

Mix together cayenne and flour.

Dip herrings into mix and coat well on all sides.

To make sauce, sweat vegetables and bay leaf in butter for few minutes.

Add white wine and reduce until almost dry.

Add fish stock and continue to reduce to almost quarter of original amount. Pour in cream and gently reheat.

Strain, return to pan and stir in mustard to taste.

Heat little butter in large frying pan and briskly fry herrings.

Meanwhile melt butter in stir-fry pan and add crushed garlic, followed by cabbage.

Stir-fry briskly for 5-8 minutes or until cabbage is softer but retains 'bite'.

Season to taste.

To Assemble

Pile cabbage in centre of dish, lay herring on top and spoon sauce over or hand around separately.

LEMON SOLE
With Brown Shrimps and Cucumber/Dill Butter Sauce

Ingredients
(Serves 4)

For the fish:

1 x 300g (11oz) lemon sole

seasoned flour for coating fish

oil or butter

For the butter sauce:

4 shallots, diced

4 tbsp dry white wine

2 tsp white wine vinegar

150ml (¼ pint) double cream

175g (6oz) unsalted butter, diced

½ cucumber

110g (4oz) brown shrimps

2 tbsp dill, chopped

Fish Method

Trim fish – cut off fins and then coat in seasoned flour on both sides.

Pat fish to remove excess flour.

Sauce Method

Heat frying pan or large saucepan.

Add shallots, white wine and wine vinegar.

Cook for 5-8 minutes on fairly brisk heat until shallots soften and wine has reduced by half.

Add cream and bring sauce to boil.

Add diced butter and whisk well.

Dice cucumber (leave on peel but don't use seeds).

Add cucumber to sauce with peeled brown shrimps.

Heat through gently and scatter in dill at last minute.

To Cook Fish

Heat large frying pan.

Add little oil or butter and cook sole, presentation side down first.

Turn over after 3-4 minutes.

Continue to cook until fish feels just soft when pressed, or edges look opaque.

Place fish on warm serving platter.

Spoon sauce around fish and garnish with few extra fronds of dill.

Serve with hot buttered new potatoes.

PERFECT FISH 'N' CHIPS

Ingredients
(Serves 4)

For the fish:

700g (1½ lb) cod or haddock fillets

2 tbsp plain flour

seasoning

8 large floury potatoes (eg Maris Piper, Arran Pilot, Cara, King Edward, Pentland Dell or Romano), peeled and cut into chips

oil for deep frying (groundnut is best but sunflower or good vegetable oil is fine)

For the batter:

225g (8oz) plain flour

½ tsp salt

300ml (½ pint) beer – dark beer will give you deep brown batter

Batter Method

Place flour and salt in large mixing bowl and make well in centre.

Pour in beer and whisk well until smooth batter, consistency of single cream, produced.

Leave to rest for 10-15 minutes.

Chips Method

Drain chips well and dry on clean tea towel or kitchen paper.

Place chips in frying basket and lower gently into oil.

Deep fry at 200°C/400°F/gas mark 6 for 6-7 minutes, until just starting to colour (This is called blanching).

Lift basket from oil.

Drain chips, then deep fry for further 3 minutes, until crisp and golden.

Drain well on kitchen paper and keep warm while frying fish.

Fish Method

Reduce heat on fryer to 190°C/375°F/gas mark 5.

Coat fish in flour and pat off excess.

Dip fish into batter and let any excess drip off.

Drop battered fish into oil very carefully.

Deep fry for about 5 minutes until crisp and golden.

Lift out fish with slotted spoon.

Drain on kitchen paper and keep warm while frying rest of fish.

Sprinkle with salt and vinegar and serve with crispy chips and mushy peas.

SARDINES *Served with Warm Tomato and Tarragon Vinaigrette*

Ingredients
(Serves 4)

For the sardines:

8 sardines, gutted and cleaned

juice of lemon

seasoning

olive oil

For the vinaigrette:

150ml ($\frac{1}{4}$ pint) olive oil

2 shallots, finely chopped

6 plum tomatoes, skinned and de-seeded.

2 tbsp freshly chopped tarragon

juice of lemon

seasoning

Method

Squeeze lemon juice over fish. Season and drizzle with olive oil.

Heat griddle pan or large frying pan.

Place sardines in pan to cook, turning over after 2-3 minutes.

In separate pan heat 150ml ($\frac{1}{4}$ pint) olive oil.

Add shallots and cook for 2 minutes.

Add tomatoes, tarragon and lemon juice. Season.

Remove fish from pan.

Place on plate and pour over sauce.

Serve with salad.

SMOKED EEL AND ASPARAGUS TARTLETS

Ingredients
(Serves 4)

225g (8oz) shortcrust pastry

2 eggs

300ml ($\frac{1}{2}$ pint) single cream

$\frac{1}{2}$ tsp cayenne pepper

salt and pepper

225g (8oz) asparagus

350g (12oz) smoked eel

225g (8oz) tinned green lentils

bunch of chives

150ml ($\frac{1}{4}$ pint) olive oil

3 tbsp balsamic vinegar

1 tbsp chopped mixed herbs
e.g. parsley/thyme/oregano

baby salad leaves

Method

Use pastry to line either large 20cm (8-inch) loose-bottomed flan tin or 4 x 10cm (4-inch) loose-bottomed tart tins.

Bake blind for 15 minutes at 190°C/375°F/gas mark 5. Cool.

Beat together eggs and single cream.

Season with cayenne and salt and pepper.

Blanch asparagus for 2-3 minutes or until just soft. Drain and cool.

Cut off and reserve tips.

Chop remaining asparagus.

Chop smoked eel and place in each of the tart cases.

Top with few asparagus spears.

Spoon some of custard mixture over eel and asparagus.

Place tarts on a baking sheet and bake at 180°C/350°F/gas mark 4 for approximately 25-30 minutes, until just set.

Meanwhile mix remaining chopped asparagus with drained tinned lentils.

Whisk up olive oil, balsamic vinegar and herbs. Season.

Toss half of dressing with lentils and asparagus.

Toss remaining dressing with leaves.

Snip chives and garnish tartlets.

To Serve

Pile leaves on plate, spoon over some lentil mixture, place tartlet on top.

Ingredients

(Serves 6)

1 x 4-5kg (9-11lb) oven-ready goose

2-3 whole onions, peeled

seasoning

For the stuffing:

225g (8oz) fresh white breadcrumbs

2 tbsp freshly chopped sage/thyme or a mixture of both

110g (4oz) onion, diced

2 cooking apples, grated

rind and juice of 2 lemons

110g (4oz) sausage meat

2 egg yolks, to bind

seasoning

For the compôte:

110g (4oz) unrefined sugar – or to taste

150ml ($\frac{1}{4}$ pint) Calvados

225g (8oz) Pruneaux d'Agen or ready-to-eat prunes

4-6 red skinned apples, cored and sliced

Goose and Stuffing Method

Pre-heat oven to 200ºC/400ºF/gas mark 6.

Place goose on rack above Basting tin.

Stuff cavity with whole onions.

Prick skin of goose all over and rub with salt.

Next make stuffing.

Place breadcrumbs in large bowl.

Add sage/thyme, onion, apples, lemon rind and juice and sausage meat.

Mix together well and bind with egg yolk.

Season well.

Stuff filling into neck end of goose.

Cook any remaining stuffing in separate dish.

Weigh goose and calculate cooking time – allow 15 minutes per pound plus 15 minutes extra.

Place goose in oven and drain off any excess fat from time to time.

Compôte Method

Place sugar in pan.

Add Calvados and prunes, followed by sliced apples.

Cook gently until apple slices have softened.

Cool.

When goose is cooked, transfer to serving platter and keep warm in low oven.

Serve with chestnuts or braised onions and green vegetable.

ROAST WILD DUCK *With Cumberland Glaze*

Ingredients
(Serves 6)

2 wild duck (or use Barbary duck)

oil

zest of 1 orange

zest of 1 lemon

juice of 2 oranges

juice of ½ lemon

55ml (2fl oz) white wine

pinch of cayenne pepper

3 tbsp redcurrant jelly

4 tbsp stock

seasoning

½ glass of port

50g (2oz) unsalted butter

1 tbsp chopped parsley

Method

Roast ducks on their legs in oil at 220°C/425°F/gas mark 7. Turn over after 10 minutes. Continue to cook for approximately 25 minutes for wild duck or 1 hour for larger ducks.

Remove from oven and leave to rest. Pour off excess oil.

Add orange and lemon zest to pan with citrus juices and white wine.

Bring to boil, reduce slightly and add cayenne pepper.

Whisk in redcurrant jelly and stock. Season to taste.

Pour sauce into roasting pan and stir well to mix in any sediment from roasted ducks.

Add port, bring to boil and whisk in butter.

Carve birds – 4 legs and 4 breasts and place skin side up on oven-proof tray.

Baste duck with half of sauce. Place under very hot grill and bubble for 5-10 minutes.

Serve glazed duck on platter and drizzle with remainder of the sauce.

Serve with roast potatoes and preferred green vegetable, garnished with chopped parsley.

Brian wades into wildfowl – and pretty wild weather – with his companions at Ely.

SAUTÉ OF CHICKEN *In Apples and Cider*

Ingredients
(Serves 6)

50g (2oz) unsalted butter

olive oil

1 large chicken or 6 chicken joints

6 dessert apples

300ml ($\frac{1}{2}$ pint) dry cider

300ml ($\frac{1}{2}$ pint) double cream

$\frac{1}{2}$ tbsp cider vinegar

2 tbsp chopped parsley

Method

Heat butter and oil together.

Joint chicken or use chicken pieces from supermarket.

Add chicken pieces, skin side down. Colour and season.

Cover and leave to cook for 20-25 minutes or until fully cooked through.

Remove from pan and keep warm.

Dice apple into 1cm ($\frac{1}{4}$-inch) pieces.

Tip excess fat from pan.

Add apples. Colour, then remove.

Add cider, bring to boil and reduce by half.

Add cream, bring to boil again and reduce until thickened.

Place chicken in sauce and reheat thoroughly. Check seasoning.

Add cider vinegar, apples and chopped parsley.

Serve with rice.

Ingredients

(Serves 4)

For the chicken:

2 tbsp sesame seed oil

2 tbsp soy sauce

4 'skin on' chicken breasts

For the vegetables:

50g (2oz) unsalted butter

2 cloves garlic, chopped

2 red chillies, de-seeded and finely chopped

1 red pepper, de-seeded and sliced

1 yellow pepper, de-seeded and sliced

1 green pepper, de-seeded and sliced

1 bunch spring onions, cut diagonally into 5cm (2 inch) lengths, including green parts

110g (4oz) mange-tout

1 tbsp soy sauce

For the chutney:

sesame oil

2 tbsp onion, chopped

1 tsp garlic, chopped

2 tbsp crystallised ginger, chopped, syrup reserved – or use fresh root ginger

2-3 tbsp raisins

1 large cooking apple, peeled and sliced

zest and juice of orange

450g (1lb) rhubarb, cut into chunks

300ml ($\frac{1}{2}$ pint) rhubarb wine

4 tbsp raspberry /red wine vinegar

50g (2oz) butter

225g (8oz) rhubarb, cut into thin batons

Chutney Method

Heat little sesame oil in large pan.

Add onion and garlic and soften for few minutes.

Next add ginger, raisins, apple, orange rind and juice and rhubarb chunks.

Give mixture good stir, then add rhubarb wine and red wine or raspberry vinegar.

Bring chutney to boil.

Reduce heat and simmer for 25-30 minutes until thick, reduced, fruity purée produced.

With remaining 50g (2oz) butter gently cook batons of rhubarb.

Add 2 tablespoons reserved syrup from ginger or use little rhubarb wine.

Stir lightly cooked batons of rhubarb into chutney and keep warm – or keep in fridge for couple of days.

Chicken Method

Mix together soy sauce and sesame seed oil.

Place chicken in shallow dish and cover with marinade.

Leave for 1 hour if possible.

Heat griddle pan or large frying pan and cook chicken breasts, skin side down, for 20-25 minutes – or until the juices run clear.

Vegetable Method

Meanwhile heat wok or stir fry pan.

Add 2oz butter.

First add garlic and chillies, then add remaining vegetables – finishing with mange tout.

Sprinkle with little soy sauce just before end of cooking time.

To Serve

Pile vegetables on plate.

Top with chicken breast and then spoonful of chutney.

CHUMP CHOP CASSEROLE
With Thyme and Garlic, served with Parsley Dumplings

Ingredients
(Serves 4)

For the dumplings:

225g (8oz) self-raising flour

110g (4oz) suet

seasoning

2 tbsp chopped parsley

5-6 tbsp cold water, to mix

For the casserole:

oil for cooking

4 x 225g (8oz) chump chops on the bone

2 large onions, chopped

1 carrot, sliced

1 leek, cleaned and sliced

4 sticks celery, sliced

25g (1oz) plain flour

6 tomatoes, de-seeded and roughly diced

900ml (1½ pints) stock

1 large glass red wine

50g (2oz) butter

4 cloves of garlic, puréed

1 bunch fresh thyme

2 tbsp chopped parsley

Dumpling Method

Place flour, suet and seasoning in large bowl, sprinkle in parsley and mix well.

Add sufficient water to make soft, but not sticky, dough.

Using floured hands, pull off small pieces of dough and roll into balls – roughly size of golf balls.

Retain for addition to casserole.

Casserole Method

Heat oil. Seal chops until coloured on both sides.

Remove and keep warm.

Add all chopped and sliced vegetables (except tomatoes) to pan.

Sauté vegetables until lightly coloured. Sprinkle in flour and stir well. Add tomatoes followed by stock and wine.

Bring mixture to boil.

Return meat to pan.

Skim any excess scum from surface.

Cover pan with lid and cook in oven at 200°C/400°F/gas mark 6 for approximately 1 hour or until meat is cooked.

Lift out meat.

Tip vegetables and stock into food processor (you may need to do this in couple of batches).

Process sauce until smooth.

Return to clean pan.

Add butter, puréed garlic and thyme. Stir well.

Return meat to pan.

Bring casserole to boil and place prepared dumplings on top.

Cover with lid and cook until dumplings have doubled in size and are nice and fluffy (this will take some 15-20 minutes).

Serve and sprinkle with parsley.

Ingredients

(Serves 8)

For the paté mixture:

450g (1lb) mushrooms, minced

25g (1oz) butter

110g (4oz) paté

seasoning

1 tbsp chopped parsley

For the pancakes:

225g (8oz) plain flour

pinch of salt

3 eggs

600ml (1 pint) milk

1 tsp vegetable oil

For the beef:

900g (2lb) fillet of beef

oil

450g (1lb) puff pastry

egg wash

Madeira sauce (A ready-made Bonne Cuisine variety from the supermarket is excellent, if you don't want to make your own)

Paté Method

Cook mushrooms in butter until dried out. Leave to cool.

Mix with paté, season and stir in chopped parsley.

Pancake Method

Sift flour and salt into bowl and form well in centre.

Add eggs, then gradually half milk, stirring constantly.

Add oil and beat well until smooth.

Add remaining milk and leave to stand for 30 minutes.

Heat 15cm (6-inch) omelette pan and add few drops of oil.

Pour in tablespoon of batter and tilt pan to coat bottom evenly.

Cook until underside is brown.

Turn over and cook underside again for about 10 seconds.

Turn out onto tea towel and cover.

Continue to make pancakes with remaining batter.

Fillet Method

Tie up beef.

Heat oil, seal fillet on all sides and leave to cool.

Roll out puff pastry to rectangular shape.

Egg wash inside area, lay pancakes all over puff pastry.

Spread mushroom mixture all over fillet.

Wrap pancakes around fillet.

Wrap pastry round meat and turn over, so that join is underneath.

Leave to rest. Decorate and eggwash.

Bake at 180°-200°C/350°-400°F/gas mark 4-6 for approximately 30 minutes.

Leave to rest. Slice and serve with Madeira sauce.

GAMMON *With a Spiced Fruit Compôte*

Ingredients
(Serves 4)

For the gammon:

4 gammon steaks

50g (2oz) butter

4 poached eggs

For the compôte:

oil

2 cloves garlic, chopped

2 tbsp root ginger, finely chopped

pinch cinnamon

pinch allspice

pinch paprika/cayenne

300ml (½ pint) apple juice

4 tbsp cider vinegar

450g (1lb) mixed ready-to-eat dried fruit
(e.g. papaya / mango / pears / prunes /
peaches / figs – or just use mix of 2-3 types
of fruit)

For the croutons:

4 slices bread, cubed

bunch of spring onions, finely sliced (use
green parts too)

oil and butter

Sweet-pickled and smoked Suffolk ham hogs the limelight at Emmett's Stores, Peasenhall.

Gammon Method
Melt butter in large frying or griddle pan.

Cook gammon steaks for 5-8 minutes each side.

Compôte Method
In separate pan heat little oil.

Add garlic and ginger and cook briefly until softened.

Add little of spices, to taste (Flavour can be adjusted as mixture begins to cook).

Add apple juice and cider vinegar followed by fruit.

Bring to the boil, then reduce heat and simmer for 20 minutes.

Meanwhile make croutons by frying cubes of bread in little oil and butter.

Toss in spring onions and continue to cook for further 3-4 minutes.

To Assemble
Place gammon steaks on plates and set poached eggs on top.

Place spoonful of compôte to one side and scatter spring onion and croutons around gammon for colour and crunch.

GRILLED BELLY OF PORK *With Horseradish Mustard*

Ingredients
(Serves 6)

25g (1oz) butter

1 belly of pork

1 onion, chopped

1 carrot, sliced

1 stick celery, sliced

1 bulb garlic, halved

4 tomatoes, halved

300ml ($\frac{1}{2}$ pint) dry white wine

1.25 litres (2 pints) brown stock

herbs – thyme, bay leaf, parsley stalks

1 small jar horseradish mustard or creamed horseradish

egg wash

225g (8oz) breadcrumbs

Method

Preheat oven to 170°C/325°F/gas mark 3.

Melt butter in frying pan and colour outside of pork.

Place in large, deep roasting dish.

In same frying pan, colour chopped onion, carrot and celery and pour over meat.

Add garlic, tomatoes, white wine and brown stock. Then add herbs.

Bake in oven for 2-3 hours.

Take out meat and slip out bones.

Leave to cool with weight on top to press down slightly.

When cold, cut on slant into strips 1cm ($\frac{1}{2}$-inch) wide.

Brush with horseradish mustard and egg wash and sprinkle with breadcrumbs.

Put in oven at 180°C/350°F/gas mark 4 to reheat thoroughly and finish under grill to colour.

Strain cooking liquor, bring to boil and serve with meat on bed of swede and carrot purée.

MEDALLIONS OF PORK
With Parsley and Sun-Dried Tomato, served with Stir Fried Vegetables

Ingredients
(Serves 6)

For the pork:

900g (2lb) piece boned loin of pork

4 eggs

300ml ($\frac{1}{2}$ pint) double cream

3 tbsp chopped parsley

4 tbsp finely grated Parmesan

4-6 pieces sun-dried tomato, drained and finely chopped

flour for dusting

seasoning

oil to shallow fry

For the vegetables:

sesame oil

2 cloves garlic, chopped

2 tbsp root ginger, chopped

selection of stir-fry vegetables (allow 110g/4oz per person) of your choice e.g. asparagus, baby corn, broccoli florets, cabbage, green beans, mange-tout.

Pork Method
Slice through pork to produce six even-sized pieces.

Place each piece between grease-proof paper or clingfilm and beat out until flattened.

Dust each 'medallion' of pork with seasoned flour, shaking off any excess.

Beat eggs and mix in cream, parsley, Parmesan and prepared sun-dried tomato pieces.

Dip each 'medallion' in batter and fry in oil for 10-15 minutes until golden brown and cooked through.

Drain on kitchen paper.

Vegetable Method
Heat little sesame oil in stir fry pan.

Add chopped garlic and ginger.

Stir fry until softened.

Add vegetables and stir fry until just softened and 'al dente'.

Serve spoonful of vegetables with golden 'medallion' of pork on top.

NEWMARKET SAUSAGES *With Chorizo and Minted Broad Beans*

Ingredients
(Serves 4)

olive oil

225g (8oz) Newmarket sausages

225g (8oz) Chorizo sausage

600ml (1 pint) brown stock

6 shallots, peeled and cut into quarters

225g (8oz) smoked bacon, diced

2 cloves garlic, sliced

150ml ($\frac{1}{4}$ pint) red wine

1 can plum tomatoes, chopped

1 can cherry tomatoes (optional)

2 tbsp fresh mint, chopped

450g (1lb) frozen broad beans, thawed and shelled

225g (8oz) pre-cooked baby new potatoes

3 tbsp chopped parsley

Method

Heat little oil in frying pan.

Colour sausages on all sides, then cover with stock, bring to boil and simmer for 5 minutes.

Drain and cool. Reserve stock.

Cut sausages into pieces approximately 5cm (2-inch) in length.

Heat little more oil, add shallots and brown lightly.

Add bacon and cook with shallots for 4-5 minutes.

Stir in garlic and sliced sausages, then red wine and plum tomatoes (and cherry tomatoes if using).

Add reserved stock, mint and shelled broad beans.

Simmer for 20-25 minutes.

Stir in new potatoes and warm through.

Sprinkle with parsley and serve with hot garlic bread, pasta or rice for hearty supper dish.

PASTA CARBONARA

Ingredients
(Serves 4)

450g (1lb) fresh or dried pasta (spinach or garlic and herb-flavoured tagliatelle works well)

olive oil

4 egg yolks

150ml ($\frac{1}{4}$ pint) double cream

50g (2oz) Parmesan cheese, finely grated – plus extra Parmesan shavings for garnish (optional)

225g (8oz) smoked streaky bacon, cut into lardons (strips)

110g (4oz) sliced chestnut or ordinary mushrooms

sprig of basil

Method

Cook pasta according to instructions on packet – remember if pasta is fresh it will only take 4 minutes or so to cook.

Drain and toss straight away in olive oil, to prevent from sticking.

Beat together egg yolks and cream. Season well and add grated Parmesan cheese.

Heat little oil in frying pan. Add streaky bacon and sauté briskly for 5 minutes.

Add mushrooms and continue to cook for further 3-4 minutes.

Drain pasta and add to pan.

Pour over cream, egg and cheese mixture and toss pasta until well coated with sauce. Heat from pasta will cook eggs.

Keep gentle heat under pan for further 3-4 minutes.

Season pasta again and pile into dish.

Sprinkle over Parmesan shavings and decorate with sprig of basil.

Serve with crispy green salad and warmed Ciabatta or Focaccia bread.

PORK FILLET *With Smoked Bacon and Spinach Risotto*

Ingredients
(Serves 4)

For the risotto:

butter and oil

1 onion, finely chopped

2 cloves garlic, chopped

225g (8oz) risotto rice

900ml (1½ pints) vegetable/chicken stock

pinch cinnamon

50g (2oz) pine nuts

110g (4oz) baby spinach, roughly chopped

For the pork:

1 x pork tenderloin fillet

2 whole rashers streaky bacon

4 rashers streaky bacon, cut into lardons (strips)

For the sauce:

rind and juice of 2 oranges

150ml (¼ pint) port

1 tbsp parsley, chopped

Risotto Method

Melt little oil and butter – about tablespoon of each – in pan.

Add onion and garlic and cook until softened.

Stir in rice and coat all grains.

Heat stock and gradually add to rice, waiting until each batch absorbed before adding next.

Add good pinch of cinnamon and pine nuts.

When all stock absorbed, risotto should be creamy.

Add chopped spinach and stir in well.

Season and leave to cool.

Pork Method

Place tenderloin on board.

Make cut all along length of the pork.

Cover with clingfilm and, using rolling pin, flatten out pork fillet.

Fill centre of the pork with cooled risotto.

Reserve remainder.

Wrap fillet with 2 rashers of bacon.

Seal all over in large pan, then roast for 25-30 minutes in hot oven at 190°C/375°F/gas mark 5.

Meanwhile, fry lardons in little oil, until just crispy.

Sauce Method

Place rind and juice of 2 oranges in pan.

Add port, bubble up and reduce by half.

Add parsley.

To Serve

Remove pork from oven and cut into pieces diagonally.

Arrange on bed of reheated reserved risotto.

Scatter lardons around fillet and serve with sauce.

RACK OF LAMB *With Mustard and Herbs*

Ingredients
(Serves 3-4)

1 rack of lamb – approximately 6-8 cutlets
French-trimmed and 'chined'

For the crust:

110g (4oz) unsalted butter

6 shallots, peeled and finely diced

110g (4oz) fresh breadcrumbs

2 tbsp chopped parsley

2 tbsp chopped rosemary

2 tbsp chopped thyme

2 tbsp Dijon mustard

seasoning

Lamb Method

Heat oven-proof pan or roasting dish.

Sear rack of lamb on all sides until just coloured.

Leave to cool.

Crust Method

Melt butter.

Add shallots and cook gently until softened but not browned.

Add breadcrumbs and herbs.

Season and mix well.

Brush cooled lamb with Dijon mustard and press in herbs.

Pat well with fingers to ensure herbs are well 'glued' to mustard.

Place in roasting dish and cook in hot oven (220°C/425°F/gas mark 7) for approximately 20-25 minutes, until pink in centre (Keep testing lamb and cook to taste).

Leave lamb to rest for 5-10 minutes.

Carve – allow 2-3 cutlets per person.

Serve with crispy roast potatoes and French beans.

As an extra touch you could melt 125g (4oz) butter and throw in 2 tbsp chopped parsley. Heat through and drizzle over the potatoes and around the lamb.

Ingredients

(Serves 6)

1.25 litre (2 pints) pie dish

For the pastry:

450g (1lb) self-raising flour

225g (8oz) beef suet

pinch of salt

water

For the filling:

2 onions, peeled and chopped

700g (1½ lb) stewing steak, cubed

225g (8oz) lambs' kidneys, quartered

few sprigs fresh thyme (or ½ tsp dried)

2 bay leaves

few sprigs fresh oregano (or ½ tsp dried)

2 tbsp Worcestershire sauce

2 tbsp mushroom ketchup

425ml (15fl oz) beef stock

225g (8oz) chestnut mushrooms, halved

1½ tbsp plain flour

For the glaze:

oil and 1 egg, beaten,

Method

Make up pastry.

Mix suet and flour together, season and add enough water to make soft but not sticky dough.

In large pan, fry onion in little oil. Then add steak and kidney and brown all over for 5-10 minutes, stirring occasionally.

Add thyme, bay leaves and oregano, followed by Worcestershire sauce and mushroom ketchup.

Gradually add stock and bring to boil, then reduce heat and simmer for 1½-2 hours, until meat is tender.

Add halved mushrooms and flour mixed to paste with a little water.

Stir stew constantly until thickened, then cool.

Meanwhile roll pastry to shape approximately 2.5cm (1-inch) larger than rim of pie dish.

Next cut pastry all round to remove 2.5cm (1-inch) strip.

Dampen edge of pie dish and press pastry strip on top.

Next dampen surface of applied strip and lay pastry lid on top, pressing down and sealing edge.

Brush pastry with beaten egg/oil to glaze and make small hole in lid to allow steam to escape.

Bake in preheated oven at 200°C/400°F/gas mark 6 for 30-40 minutes, until golden brown.

APPLE JACKS

Dumplings weren't always eaten as a savoury. They were eaten as a sweet course too – sometimes served with sugar and butter, or with treacle.

In East Anglia there was a very popular apple dumpling – better known in Norfolk as Apple Johns or Apple Jacks.

Ingredients
(Serves 4)

225g (8oz) chilled shortcrust pastry

For the filling:

4 cooking apples

1 tbsp lemon juice

25g (1oz) Demerera sugar

25g (1oz) butter, diced

50g (2oz) raisins

½ tsp mixed spice

For the glaze:

1 lightly beaten egg white

caster sugar

Method

Peel and core apples and brush with lemon juice to prevent browning.

Mix together sugar, butter, raisins and mixed spice.

Place dough on floured board and divide into 4.

Roll out each piece to 15cm (6-inch) square.

Place one apple in middle of each pastry square.

Fill centre of apple with raisin mixture.

Brush edges of pastry with water, then draw up over apple to enclose completely.

Place apple jack on greased baking sheet.

Brush with egg white and dredge with caster sugar.

Bake in hot oven 200°C/400°F/gas mark 6 for 40-45 minutes or until pastry is golden brown.

Serve with custard.

BEDFORDSHIRE WIGS

Ingredients
(Makes approximately 24)

450g (1lb) black treacle

110g (4oz) butter

300ml (½ pint) milk

110g (4oz) caster sugar

1 tsp bicarbonate of soda

450g (1lb) plain flour

2 level tsp ground ginger

10g (½ oz) caraway seeds (optional)

Method

Grease tray of individual Yorkshire pudding tins or line with muffin papers.

Heat oven to 180°C/350°F/gas mark 4.

Melt treacle and butter. Stir in milk, sugar, bicarbonate of soda, flour and ginger (and caraway seeds, if using).

Beat mixture well and divide between tins.

Bake for 30 minutes or until mixture has risen and fanned 'wig' around edges of tin.

Early trifles were made with a syllabub topping instead of the whipped, sweetened cream we have nowadays.

The following recipe is a guide. It's really up to you if you want to add a little more booze or fruit – and you can alter the proportions to suit the size of your trifle dish, or the size of your party.

However you make it, the trifle remains the traditional centrepiece of many celebratory tables.

Ingredients

(Serves a generous 4)

For the trifle base:

8 trifle sponges, cut in half – or dozen macaroon biscuits

300ml ($\frac{1}{2}$ pint) medium sherry

150ml ($\frac{1}{4}$ pint) brandy

225g (8oz) fresh or frozen raspberries or a packet of frozen mixed berries – thawed

600ml (1 pint) thick, smooth custard

75g (3oz) flaked almonds

For the syllabub:

150ml ($\frac{1}{4}$ pint) white wine

1 tbsp dry sherry

zest and juice of lemon

50g (2oz) caster sugar

300ml ($\frac{1}{2}$ pint) double or whipping cream

Method

Place trifle sponges or macaroons in base of trifle dish.

Sprinkle with 300ml ($\frac{1}{2}$ pint) sherry and 150ml ($\frac{1}{4}$ pint) brandy and leave to soak while whipping up syllabub, as follows:

Pour 150ml ($\frac{1}{4}$ pint wine) and tbsp sherry into basin.

Add zest and juice of lemon.

Leave for few hours or overnight if possible.

Strain and discard zest. Reserve liquid.

Add sugar to wine mixture and stir until dissolved.

Add cream and whip with balloon whisk, until mixture just holds its shape and hangs from whisk.

Place fruit over macaroons.

Next pour custard over, followed by whipped cream/syllabub mixture.

Scatter with few reserved macaroons and/or flaked almonds.

For special occasions trifle could be decorated with gold or silver almonds or flaked chocolate.

CAKES, TARTS AND PUDDINGS

BUCKINGHAMSHIRE CHERRY BUMPERS

The Black Cherry Orchards of Buckinghamshire were once famous for the delicious fruit picking that took place during late summer, culminating in Cherry Pie Sunday at the end of August.

An inn at Cadsden, near Princes Risborough, used to sell many Cherry Bumpers with a pint of ale!

You can try them hot or cold with good thick custard or clotted cream.

Ingredients
(Serves 4)

225g (8oz) shortcrust pastry

450g (1lb) black cherries – fresh or tinned
(if tinned, drain really well)

50g (2oz) granulated sugar (optional)

caster sugar for sprinkling

egg for brushing (optional)

Method

Heat oven to 200°C/400°F/gas mark 6.

Roll out pastry to about 8mm ($\frac{1}{4}$-inch) thickness and cut into 10cm (4-inch) circles.

Stone cherries – if fresh sprinkle with sugar.

Pile some cherries into centre of each pastry circle.

Brush edges with water or use beaten egg.

Fold pastry circles, pressing edges together to form half moon shape, and flute attractively.

Brush with little water or beaten egg and sprinkle with caster sugar.

Bake for 20-25 minutes until lightly golden brown.

CATTERN CAKES

Ingredients
(Makes approximately 15)

250g (9oz) self raising flour

$\frac{1}{4}$ tsp cinnamon

25g (1oz) currants

50g (2oz) ground almonds

2 tsp caraway seeds (optional)

200g (7oz) caster sugar

110g (4oz) melted butter

1 egg beaten

extra sugar and cinnamon to sprinkle over surface

Method

Sift flour and cinnamon into large mixing bowl.

Stir in currants, almonds, caraway seeds (if using) and sugar.

Add melted butter and beaten egg and mix to soft dough.

Roll out to 30cm x 25cm (12 x 10-inch) rectangle.

Brush lightly with little water.

Sprinkle with little extra sugar and cinnamon.

Roll up like Swiss roll and cut into 2cm ($\frac{3}{4}$-inch) slices.

Place well apart on greased baking trays.

Bake for 10-15 minutes at 190°C/375°F/gas mark 5 or until golden brown and fully cooked through.

Syllabub has been a favourite since Elizabethan times – the word 'bub' was slang for fizzy wine or latter day bubbly.
Originally syllabub was a drink made by milking a cow directly into a bucket of beer, wine or cider.
Charles II was a particular fan and kept in St James Park a herd of cows milked by beautiful girls whose complexions
were radiantly clear because their contact with the cows kept them free from smallpox. In Norfolk syllabub was traditionally
made with cider but, in this version from Essex, it's made with sweet white wine.

Ingredients

(Serves 2 large portions or four small)

150ml ($\frac{1}{4}$ pint) white wine

1 tbsp medium dry sherry

2 tbsp brandy

zest and juice of 1 lemon

50g (2oz) caster sugar

300ml ($\frac{1}{2}$ pint) double cream

110g (4oz) fresh raspberries – or defrosted frozen

icing sugar (optional)

broken cinnamon stick/rosemary sprig – to decorate.

Method

Pour wine, sherry and brandy into basin.

Add zest and lemon juice to wine mixture. Leave for few hours or overnight if possible. Strain out and discard zest.

Add sugar to wine mixture and stir until dissolved.

Add cream and whip with balloon whisk until mixture thickens and holds its shape.

Using fork, press raspberries and sweeten if necessary with little icing sugar.

Divide raspberries between sundae dishes and fold rest into cream mixture.

Pile syllabub into glasses.

Chill and decorate with broken cinnamon stick and rosemary.

FENLAND APPLE CAKE

A crisp pastry case, filled with juicy marrow and apple and topped with cake crumbs.
A Million was a type of marrow which used to be treated as a fruit, not a vegetable.

Because of its size, a marrow was a useful bulky ingredient for hungry families and its rather bland flavour was counteracted by a selection of well used spices of the time – nutmeg, mixed spice or cinnamon.

Ingredients
(Serves 6)

For the spiced cream:

300ml ($\frac{1}{2}$ pint) double cream

$\frac{1}{4}$ tsp mixed spice or cinnamon

For the apple cake:

1 x 20cm (8-inch) pastry case

900g (2lb) Bramley apples, peeled, cored and sliced

225g (8oz) vegetable marrow, peeled, de-seeded and cut into chunks

50g (2oz) butter

110g (4oz) caster sugar (or to taste)

good pinch of nutmeg, cinnamon or mixed spice

75g (3oz) cake crumbs e.g. Madeira

Method

Whip cream until just 'hanging' from whisk and looking thick and floppy.

Gently fold in mixed spice or cinnamon and chill well.

Line 20cm (8-inch) loose-bottomed flan tin with pastry and bake 'blind' for 10-15 minutes, covering pastry with grease-proof paper and baking beans.

Remove baking beans and grease-proof paper and place tart back in oven for further 5-10 minutes to dry out and colour slightly.

Place prepared apples and marrow in saucepan with butter.

Sprinkle in sugar and spice.

Cook, stirring frequently, until apple and marrow mixture becomes soft and pulpy. Place in pastry case.

Scatter over cake crumbs, place in hot oven at 190°C/375°F/gas mark 5 and heat through for 10 minutes.

Serve apple cake with spiced whipped cream and a sprig or two of mint.

Ginger has always been one of the most popular English spices. It is believed to aid digestion and is also warming in a cold climate.

Many counties share recipes for gingerbread but this version has special links with Colchester – where there is an annual tradition of toasting the start of the oyster season with a glass of gin and a slice.

Ingredients

(Serves 12)

For the gingerbread:

350g (12oz) plain flour

175g (6oz) butter

1½ tsp ground ginger

2 level tsp cinnamon

pinch nutmeg

1 level tsp bicarbonate of soda

4 tbsp milk

175g (6oz) black treacle

175g (6oz) golden syrup

175g (6oz) soft brown sugar

2 eggs, beaten

For the spiced plums:

25g (1oz) butter

50g (2oz) unrefined soft brown sugar

30ml (2 tbsp) red wine

225g (8oz) plums, stoned and halved

½ tsp nutmeg

½ tsp cinnamon

Gingerbread Method

Line base and sides of 20cm (8-inch) square tin with grease-proof paper.

Sift flour and spices into large bowl.

Mix bicarbonate of soda with milk and leave to one side.

Measure black treacle, syrup, butter and sugar into large saucepan.

Add 150ml (¼ pint) cold water and heat gently – but do not allow to boil.

Add syrup mixture to dry flour mix and beat until smooth.

Next add beaten eggs, little at time, followed by milk and bicarbonate of soda.

Pour mixture into tin and bake at 170ºC/325ºF/gas mark 3 for 1¼-1½ hours, until cake is risen and firm to touch.

Cool in tin.

Serve in slices with spiced plums.

Spiced Plums Method

Melt butter in saucepan.

Add sugar and wine and heat.

Add plums and spices.

Cover and simmer until plums are softened.

Serve with gingerbread and spoonful of clotted cream.

Ingredients

(Serves 6)

For the pudding:

450ml (¾ pint) full cream milk

150ml (¼ pint) double cream

50g (2oz) fresh white breadcrumbs

75g (3oz) caster sugar

175g (6oz) ground almonds

1 tsp orange flower water or rose water

3 eggs, separated

75g (3oz) caster sugar

25g (1oz) butter

50g (2oz) flaked almonds

For the compôte:

8 oranges, peeled thickly

300ml (½ pint) water/wine

110g (4oz) caster sugar

2 tbsp Grand Marnier (optional)

Pudding Method

Warm milk and cream in pan.

Place breadcrumbs in bowl and add milk and cream mixture.

Leave to stand for 5 minutes.

Add sugar, ground almonds and orange flower water.

Leave to stand for further 10 minutes or until all liquid absorbed.

Stir in egg yolks.

Pour mixture into buttered pie dish and dot surface with butter.

Set dish in Bain Marie.

Bake for 30 minutes at 180°C/350°F/gas mark 4 or until set and golden brown.

Meanwhile, in clean bowl, whisk up egg whites to soft peak.

Whisk in half second amount of sugar then fold in rest.

Pile meringue on set pudding.

Scatter with almonds and brown in oven at 220°C/425°F/gas mark 7 for 8-10 minutes.

Compôte Method

Segment oranges and retain juice.

Place juice plus wine and water in pan with sugar.

Heat gently and reduce by one third. Cool.

Add orange segments and stir in Grand Marnier, if desired.

Ingredients

(Makes 4-6 individual tarts or 1 large 20cm/8-inch flan)

225g (8oz) made shortcrust pastry – or use bought variety.

50g (2oz) unsalted butter, softened

50g (2oz) caster sugar

$\frac{1}{2}$ tsp ground nutmeg

2 tbsp fresh white breadcrumbs

2 eggs, lightly beaten

225g (8oz) sieved curd cheese – or use cream cheese or Mascarpone

juice $\frac{1}{2}$ lemon

rind of whole lemon

50g (2oz) currants

Method

Heat oven to 190°C/375°F/gas mark 5.

Roll out pastry and line tart tins.

Mix together butter, sugar, nutmeg and breadcrumbs.

Stir in eggs, cheese and lemon rind, mixing well.

Finally, stir in lemon juice and currants.

Divide mixture between pastry cases and bake for 20-25 minutes – or until mixture is set and light golden brown.

Dust with icing sugar and serve with clotted cream and sprig of mint.

Delicious either hot or cold.

NELSON SLICES

Most counties have their own version of bread pudding, eaten either as a pudding with custard or cut into squares and eaten as a cake.
In Norfolk it's often known as Nelson Cake or Nelson Slices in memory of Admiral Lord Nelson, who was born in the county.

Ingredients
(Serves 6)

8 slices medium bread

300ml ($\frac{1}{2}$ pint) milk

350g (12oz) mixed dried fruit

50g (2oz) mixed chopped peel

1 eating apple, grated

3 tbsp soft dark brown sugar

2 tbsp dark marmalade

40g (1$\frac{1}{2}$oz) self raising flour

2 eggs

juice of lemon

1 tsp cinnamon

110g (4oz) butter

icing sugar

Method

Break up bread, including crusts, and soak in milk until soft.

Beat well until mixture is like soft cream.

Add dried fruit, peel and apple.

Stir in sugar, marmalade, flour, eggs, lemon juice and cinnamon.

Melt butter and pour half into mixture.

Beat well and pour into greased 28cm x 20cm (11 x 8-inch) roasting tin.

Pour remaining butter in thin stream over surface.

Bake at 150°C/300°F/gas mark 2 for 1$\frac{1}{2}$ hours and then for 30 minutes at 180°C/350°F/gas mark 4.

Cut into squares and serve hot or cold sprinkled with icing sugar.

CAKES, TARTS AND PUDDINGS

NORFOLK TREACLE TART

Norfolk and Suffolk share a special recipe, recorded in many hand-written recipe books, for treacle tart.

Suffolk's version omits the cream and is often known as treacle custard because, unlike the traditional version, it doesn't contain any breadcrumbs and is less sweet, rich and cloying.

Before the arrival of golden syrup in the 1880s, black treacle would have been used instead.

Ingredients
(Serves 6)

225g (8oz) shortcrust pastry

7 tbsp golden syrup

grated rind and juice of 1 lemon

20g ($\frac{3}{4}$ oz) unsalted butter, melted

2-3 tbsp single cream

2 eggs, beaten

Method

Heat oven to 180°C/350°F/gas mark 4.

Grease 20cm (8-inch) flan tin or pie plate and line with pastry.

Prick base lightly and bake blind with grease-proof paper and pastry beans for 10-15 minutes.

Warm syrup in pan and stir in lemon rind and juice, butter and cream.

Beat eggs and strain through sieve into syrup mixture. Stir to mix well.

Pour into pastry case and bake for 30-35 minutes or until filling is lightly set.

Serve warm or cold with custard or cream.

TRINITY BURNT CREAM (CRÈME BRÛLÉE)

This dessert is otherwise known as Trinity Pudding, or Trinity Cream, after the Cambridge College.

Legend has it that the recipe was brought to Trinity College by an undergraduate in the 1860s. Although his initial attempt to add it to the menu was rejected by the college kitchens, he eventually became a fellow and had his way.

The pudding became a great favourite and is served at the college to this day.

Ingredients
(Serves 6)

8 egg yolks

50g (2oz) caster sugar

1 vanilla pod (or few drops vanilla extract)

600ml (1 pint) double cream

icing sugar/caster sugar for dusting

Method

Heat oven to 180°C/350°F/gas mark 4.

Mix egg yolks and 50g (2oz) sugar in bowl.

If using vanilla pod, place in saucepan with cream and bring to boil.

Remove pod and scrape seeds into cream.

Whisk cream into egg yolks and sugar.

Place bowl over pan of hot water and heat until custard begins to thicken, stirring all the time – it should be the consistency of single cream.

Divide between six 7.5cm (3-inch) ramekins.

Place dishes in roasting tin and pour in enough warm water to come halfway up sides.

Cook in oven for 20-30 minutes or until custard is just set.

Remove from oven and cool.

Sprinkle with either icing or caster sugar and place under hot grill until sugar bubbles and begins to caramelise.

Cool and serve.

WALNUT BREAD
Served with Apple and Walnut Marmalade

Ingredients

(Serves 4)

For the walnut bread:

1 x 7g ($\frac{1}{4}$ oz) sachet of easy blend yeast

450g (1lb) strong white flour (or use flour of your choice, perhaps a mixture of wholegrain and white)

240ml (8fl oz) milk and water mixed – hand hot

$\frac{1}{2}$ level tsp salt

110g (4oz) roughly chopped walnuts

olive oil

For the apple and walnut marmalade:

1kg ($2\frac{1}{4}$ lb) eating apples, cored and cut into 8

rind and juice of 2 lemons

125g (4oz) light Muscovado sugar

50g (2oz) unsalted butter

pinch grated nutmeg

125g (4oz) walnuts, roughly chopped

Based on an original recipe devised by Lesley Waters

Walnut Bread Method

Sprinkle sachet of yeast into flour in warmed mixing bowl.

Add salt and stir well.

Gradually add water, oil and milk mixture to flour to produce soft, but not sticky, dough.

Turn out onto floured board and knead for 10 minutes.

Finally place in clean bowl and cover with tea towel.

Leave to rise until doubled in bulk.

Knock back mixture when doubled in size, then work in walnuts.

Shape dough into rounds or place in loaf tins and cover again.

Leave to prove for about half an hour.

Bake in hot oven (200°C/400°F/gas mark 6) for 25-30 minutes – or until loaf sounds hollow when base is lightly tapped.

Serve with apple and walnut marmalade.

Apple and Walnut Marmalade Method

Place apples, lemon rind and juice in pan.

Stir in sugar, butter and nutmeg.

Cover with sheet of crumpled, dampened grease-proof paper and lid.

Cook very gently until fruit just soft.

Remove grease-proof paper and increase heat.

Cook until mixture thickens and excess liquid reduced.

Cool slightly and stir in walnuts.

Spoon into pretty container and serve with walnut bread and good local cheese.

WALSINGHAM HONEY CAKE

Little Walsingham is a busy pilgrimage centre which has a long history of bee-keeping,
producing some excellent honey.

This is just one of many delicious recipes using this local produce – although you can, of
course, use any runny honey you choose.

Ingredients

For the cake:

225g (8oz) unsalted butter

225g (8oz) light Muscovado sugar

300ml ($\frac{1}{2}$ pint) milk

75g (3oz) black treacle

75g (3oz) runny honey

2 eggs

450g (1lb) plain flour

1 level tsp ground ginger

1 level tsp bicarbonate of soda

50g (2oz) candied peel, chopped

50g (2oz) glacé cherries, cut in half

50g (2oz) seedless raisins

For the topping:

4 tbsp runny honey

40g (1$\frac{1}{2}$ oz) light Muscovado sugar

50g (2oz) unsalted butter

50g (2oz) flaked almonds.

Cake Method

Heat oven to 160ºC/325ºF/gas mark 3.

Grease and base line 900g (2lb) loaf tin.

Cream together butter and sugar until light and fluffy.

Place milk, treacle and honey in pan and heat gently until lukewarm.

Beat into creamed mixture with eggs.

Sieve together flour, ginger and bicarbonate of soda and beat into mixture.

Stir in peel, cherries and raisins.

Pour mixture into tin and bake for 2-2$\frac{1}{2}$ hours until skewer inserted into centre of cake comes out clean.

Topping Method

Warm together honey, butter and sugar, until just melted.

Spread mixture over warm cake.

Sprinkle with flaked almonds.

In Bedfordshire there used to be a two-day fair, the highlight of which was the sale of baked pears – known as 'Wardens'.
The pears were sold from large earthenware dishes and accompanied by the following rhyme:

"Smoking hot, piping hot

Who knows what I've got

In my pot? Hot baked Wardens

All hot! All hot! All hot!"

Of course, the pears are just as delicious cold - and you don't have to sing for your supper!

Ingredients

(Serves 6)

6 large firm pears

lemon juice

450ml ($\frac{3}{4}$ pint) red wine – or enough to cover pears

50g (2oz) dark Muscovado sugar

pinch cinnamon

pinch ground ginger

pinch saffron

Method

Peel pears and brush with lemon juice to prevent browning.

Cut slice from base and stand pears in pan.

Mix together wine and sugar, whisk in spices and pour over pears.

Cover and bring to boil, then simmer until pears are just softened.

You may need to keep drizzling pears with wine as they cook.

If you want very red colour, add 2-3 drops of red food colouring.

Serve with lightly whipped cream and mint leaves.

NB The amount of sugar is a guide. You can increase the amount depending on how sweet a tooth you have.

Locations, food suppliers and organisations featured in the series

SPRING SERIES

Programme links and pudding recipes filmed at Sulgrave Manor, Sulgrave, Banbury, Oxfordshire OX17 2SD – Tel. 01295 760205; Fax. 01295 768056.

This home of George Washington's ancestors is open to the public from the beginning of April to the end of October.

On weekdays (Wednesdays excepted) the hours are from 2.00pm-5.30pm, extended to include mornings from 10.30am-1.00pm at weekends, on Bank Holidays, during the month of August and on December 27th and 30th.

In March, November and December the afternoon opening is cut back to 2.00pm-4.30pm.

Sulgrave is closed on December 25th, 26th and 31st as well as for the whole of January and is open to pre-booked schools and groups only in February.

There are a number of special events – many of them with an historical theme – throughout the year and admission for these is: Adults £4.50, children (age 5-16) £2.25 and family ticket (two adults and two or more children) £12.00. Admission at other times is adults £3.75 and children £1.75.

Oyez, Oyez – The Town Crier samples Brian's Norfolk Dumplings at Swaffham Market.

PROGRAMME ONE

Maldon Crystal Salt Company Ltd, The Downs, Maldon, Essex CM9 5HR (Tel. 01621 853315) make the famous Maldon Sea Salt.

Brian's traditional Norfolk Dumplings were made on Swaffham Market, held every Saturday.

He cooked his casserole with dumplings at Strattons Hotel, 4 Ash Close, Swaffham, Norfolk PE37 7NH (Tel. 01760 723845; Fax. 01760 720458).

PROGRAMME TWO

Coles Traditional Foods, Station Approach, Great Chesterford, Saffron Waldon, Essex CB10 1PG (Tel. 01799 531053; Fax 01799 531140) make Elizabethan saffron cakes and much else besides.

Brian cooked at The Saffron Hotel, 10 High Street, Saffron Walden CB11 1AY (Tel. 01799 522676).

He went shooting with Ely and District Wildfowling Association, which can be contacted via Derek Robinson of Burleigh House, 23 Hereward Street, March, Cambridgeshire PE15 8LZ (Tel. 01354 655599) and then cooked at The Anchor Inn, Bury Lane, Sutton Gault, Sutton, near Ely CB6 2BD (Tel. 01353 778537).

PROGRAMME THREE

Aspall of The Cyder House, Aspall Hall, Debenham, Stowmarket, Suffolk IP14 6PD (Tel. 01728 860510) make traditional cyder, apple juice and cyder vinegar. Much of their produce is organic.

Thetford Warren Lodge – featured in the rabbits item – is an ancient monument owned by English Heritage. It is open to the public and is signposted off the Thetford to Brandon road two miles outside Thetford.

PROGRAMME FOUR

Elsenham Quality Foods Ltd, Gaunts End, Bishop's Stortford, Herts CM22 6DT (Tel. 01279 812442) make jams, preserves, mustards and Gentleman's Relish.

Brian cooked at the Whitehall Hotel, Church End, Broxted, Essex CM6 2BZ (Tel. 01279 850603).

Brian shows he's game for a pheasant shoot on a Norfolk farm.

Gunns Bakery, 8 Market Square, Sandy, Bedfordshire SG19 1HU (Tel. 01767 680434) is a general bakery which also makes Bedfordshire Clangers.

The Shuttleworth Collection, Old Warden Aerodrome, near Biggleswade, Bedfordshire SG18 9EP (Tel. 01767 627288) is home to a large collection of historic aeroplanes and vehicles, including the traction engine seen in the programme.

Brian cooked at Shuttleworth College, Old Warden Park, Biggleswade, Bedfordshire SG18 9EA (Tel. 01767 626200), which is an agricultural college. Its restaurant is open to the public during the summer season, as it serves the neighbouring Swiss Garden.

PROGRAMME FIVE

The Mustard Shop, 3 Bridewell Alley, Norwich NR2 1AQ (Tel. 01603 627889) is part shop and part museum. It houses a fine collection of Colmans memorabilia as well as selling an extensive range of powdered and prepared mustards.

Brian cooked at The Old Mill Restaurant, Mill Road, Stoke Holy Cross, Norwich NR14 8PA (Tel. 01508 493337), which occupies the site of the original Colmans flour mill.

Herrings came from J T Cole's smokehouses at Newcombe Road, Lowestoft (Tel. 01502 574446), which sell on a wholesale basis.

The Cole connection continued with Donny Cole's pub – The Swan Inn at Swan Lane, Barnby, Beccles, Suffolk NR34 7QF (Tel. 01502 476646) – where Brian cooked.

PROGRAMME SIX

The Parson Woodforde Society can be contacted via The Secretary at 76 Spencer Street, Norwich, and the Parson Woodforde pub is at Church Street, Weston Longville, Norwich, Norfolk NR9 5JU (Tel. 01603 880106).

Philip Blake, The Market, Great Yarmouth, is a pork butcher specialising in sausages, jot, pigs' fry and brawn.

Brian cooked at The Imperial Hotel, North Drive, Great Yarmouth NR30 1EQ (Tel. 01493 851113).

AUTUMN SERIES

Programme links and traditional pudding recipes filmed at Oxburgh Hall (National Trust), Oxborough, King's Lynn, Norfolk PE33 9PS – Administrator Tel. 01366 328258; Restaurant Tel. 01366 328243.

PROGRAMME ONE

Featured were Pakenham Water Mill, which can be found at Pakenham in Suffolk (Tel. 01359 230275), and The Metfield Bakery, which operates on a wholesale basis but also sells through a retail outlet – Metfield Stores, Harleston, Norfolk IP20 0LB (Tel. 01379 586798).

PROGRAMME TWO

The Norfolk Nobs item was filmed at Merv's Hot Bread Kitchen, 38 Market Place, Wymondham, Norwich, Norfolk NR18 0DF (Tel. 01953 607118) and Norfolk Rural Life Museum, Beech House, Gressenhall, East Dereham, Norfolk NR20 4DR (Tel. 01362 860563), where the Norfolk Apples and Orchards Project can be contacted.

The rare breeds item was filmed at Wimpole Home Farm (National Trust), Wimpole Hall, Old Wimpole Road, Arrington, near Royston, Cambs SG8 0BW (Tel. 01223 207257) and with Peter Cruickshank, 124 Wulfstan Way, Cambridge CB1 4QJ (Tel. 01223 566054), who is a butcher registered under the Rare Breeds Accreditation scheme for Cambridgeshire.

PROGRAMME THREE

Featured Buckden Wine and Beermakers' Society, which can be contacted via 41 Manor Gardens, Buckden, Huntingdon PE18 9TN.

"Make mine chine," says Brian – preferably the Lincolnshire stuffed variety on sale at Parkinson's of Crowland!

Brian cooked at The Lion Hotel, High Street, Buckden, Huntingdon, Cambs PE18 9XA (Tel. 01480 810313).

PROGRAMME FOUR

The Suffolk ham item involved Emmetts Stores, High Street, Peasenhall, Saxmundham, Suffolk IP17 2HJ (Tel. 01728 660250), which is famous for its sweet-pickled and smoked ham and bacon, made to a traditional Suffolk recipe. A mail order service is available.

Brian cooked at Weavers Tea Rooms, 2 The Knoll, Peasenhall, Suffolk IP17 2JE (Tel. 01728 660548).

PROGRAMME FIVE

The Newmarket sausages item featured Hall Farm Fine Produce, 1 The Rookery, Newmarket, Suffolk CB8 8EQ (Tel. 01638 661824), which sells Musks Newmarket Sausages.

Other locations were Powters (pork shop), Wellington Street, Newmarket CB8 0HT (Tel. 01638 662418) and Eric Tennant (Butchers), 11 The Rookery, Newmarket, Suffolk CB8 8EQ (Tel. 01638 661530).

The seafood item was filmed with A & M Frary Sea Foods, The Quayside, Wells-next-the-Sea, Norfolk, which sells a wide selection of local shellfish – including brown shrimps, cockles, crabs, lobsters and whelks.

PROGRAMME SIX

Featured River Farm Smokery, Bottisham (at the junction of Wilbraham Road on the A1303), Cambridgeshire CB5 9BU (Tel. 01223 812577), which sells all manner of smoked meat and fish products – including chicken breasts, eels, salmon and trout.

Brian cooked at Oliver Cromwell's House/Museum – which also houses the local Tourist Information Centre – at 29 St Mary's Street, Ely CB7 4HF (Tel. 01353 662062).

The Tolly Cobbold Brewery and Brewery Tap pub can be found at Cliff Quay, Ipswich, Suffolk IP3 0AZ. Tours of the brewery can be arranged by telephoning 01473 281508.

PROGRAMME SEVEN

The Crowland butcher featured was Parkinson's, 6 West Street, Crowland, Lincolnshire PE6 0ED (Tel. 01733 210233), which makes and sells traditional Lincolnshire pork sausages, brawn and stuffed chine and was presented with the Best Butcher in Britain Award 1999 by Country Living magazine.

Crowland Abbey, which this year celebrates its 1300th anniversary, is open to the public daily.

The British Goose Producers' Association can be contacted via John Adlard, Norfolk Geese, Chestnut Farm, Pulham Market, Diss, Norfolk IP21 4XG (Tel. 01379 676391; Fax. 01379 676451).

Brian cooked for this programme at the Fox and Goose Inn, Fressingfield, near Eye, Suffolk IP21 5PB (Tel. 01379 586247).

Brian takes a gander at John Adlard's Norfolk Geese.

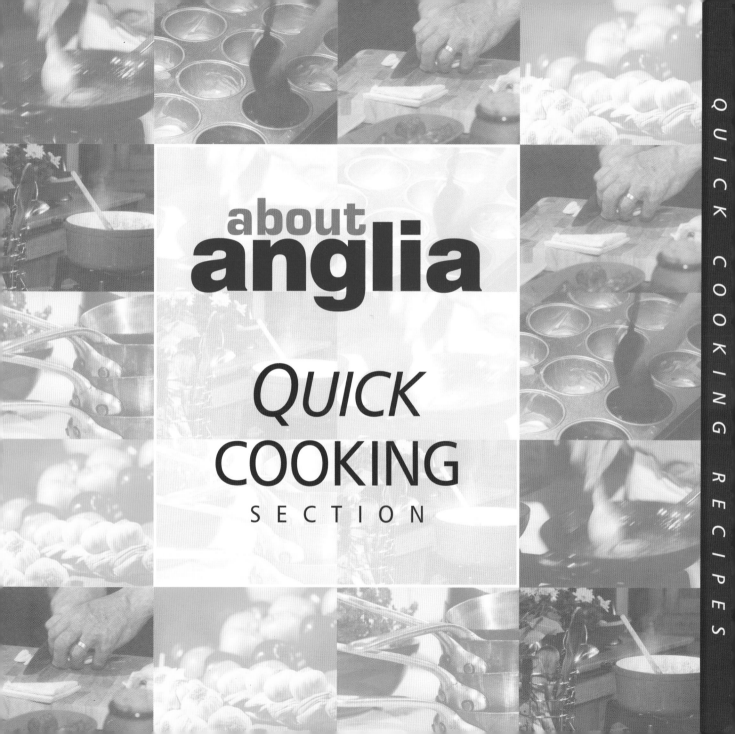

about
anglia

QUICK
COOKING
S E C T I O N

pasta primavera

Ingredients
(Serves 4)

400g (14oz) dried tagliatelle or pappardelle

1 tbsp olive oil

1 onion, peeled and chopped

1 red pepper, cored and sliced

1 yellow pepper, cored and sliced

1 green pepper, cored and sliced

2 courgettes, trimmed and cut into julienne strips

250ml (8fl oz) double cream

4 tbsp freshly-grated Parmesan cheese

2 tbsp freshly-chopped herbs – parsley, chervil, chives or dill (if available)

salt and pepper

Method
Cook pasta, following manufacturer's guidelines.

Meanwhile, heat oil in wok or large frying pan.

Stir fry vegetables for 2-3 minutes (or until at level of tenderness required).

Pour in cream and heat through gently.

Remove from heat and stir in Parmesan cheese.

Drain pasta and transfer to large warm serving bowl.

Pour vegetables and sauce over pasta, sprinkle with herbs – and more Parmesan cheese, if desired.

Toss well and serve at once.

crusty baked haddock
with sauté potatoes and bacon

Ingredients
(Serves 4)

4 x 175-225g (6-8oz) haddock fillets

25-40g (1-1½ oz) butter

½ small onion, very finely chopped

150g (5oz) fresh breadcrumbs

2 heaped tbsp chopped fresh parsley

salt and pepper

1 tbsp olive oil

350g (12oz) potatoes, diced

110g (4oz) smoked bacon, diced

Method
Pre-heat grill to medium.

Melt butter in pan, add onion and cook gently for 2-3 minutes, or until softened.

Turn onions out into bowl. Add breadcrumbs and parsley, season with salt and pepper and mix together well all ingredients.

Place haddock fillets on lightly-greased baking tray.

Coat top of each fillet with crumb mixture, pressing down firmly to develop good crust.

Place fillets under grill, not too close to heat, and cook for about ten minutes – until fish has milky white texture and crust has turned golden brown.

While fish is cooking, heat tablespoon of oil in frying pan.

Add potato and sauté until tender.

About half way through add bacon and sauté this too, stirring occasionally.

Serve crusted fish on bed of sautéed bacon and potato – and, possibly, a squeeze of lemon.

salmon fish cakes
with garlic roast tomatoes

Ingredients
(Serves 4)

For the salmon fish cakes:

1 tbsp olive oil

1 small onion, finely chopped

225g (8oz) freshly cooked salmon or canned red salmon

225g (8oz) mashed potato

1 tsp anchovy essence (optional)

plain flour for coating

1 egg, beaten

75g (3oz) fresh brown breadcrumbs

salt and pepper

cooking oil for frying

For the garlic roast tomatoes:

225g (8oz) fresh tomatoes

2 tbsp olive oil

2 cloves garlic, finely chopped

zest of one lemon

Fish Cake Method

Sauté onion in oil until tender.

Discard any skin and bones from salmon.

Mix together salmon and mashed potato. Add sautéed onion and anchovy essence (if using). Season well.

Divide mixture evenly and form into individual cake shapes.

Dip each cake into beaten egg, then roll in breadcrumbs. Repeat for a thicker, crunchier finish.

Heat oil in large frying pan (enough to cover base).

Cook fishcakes for about 3 minutes on each side, or until piping hot in centre and golden brown and crunchy on outside.

Serve with tartare sauce and lemon wedges, or with roast tomatoes (as below).

Garlic Roast Tomatoes Method

Cut tomatoes into quarters and place in ovenware dish.

Drizzle over olive oil to coat. Sprinkle over chopped garlic and lemon zest.

Bake in oven at 180°C/350°F/gas mark 4 for 20-25 minutes until softened.

warm salad of griddled scallops

Ingredients
(Serves 4 as starter; 2 as main course)

12 large scallops

6 rashers streaky bacon, de-rinded

lime/lemon wedges

For the dressing:

2 tsp Dijon mustard

1 tsp caster sugar

juice of one lemon

2 tbsp wine vinegar

8 tbsp good quality olive oil

pinch sea salt

black pepper

mixed salad leaves

Method

Prepare scallops – remove from shell, if necessary. Trim and remove any black pieces.

Wrap each scallop tightly in streaky bacon.

Heat griddle pan and cook scallops, 2-3 minutes on each side until soft and juicy.

Meanwhile, make dressing by whisking together all ingredients.

To serve, pile salad leaves onto plate. Arrange scallops, then spoon over dressing.

Serve with crusty bread for light but delicious supper dish.

quick thai curry

Ingredients
(Serves 4)

oil for cooking

4 skinless chicken breasts

1 large onion, diced

2 cloves garlic, crushed

2-3 tbsp red Thai curry paste (according to taste) from packet or jar

400ml (13fl oz) can coconut milk

225g (8oz) Thai jasmine rice

handful fresh coriander

toasted almond flakes to garnish

Method

Heat oil in wok or large frying pan.

Add garlic and onion and cook until softened. Cut chicken into bite-sized pieces. Place in pan and cook for 5 minutes or so until lightly browned on all sides.

Stir in Thai paste and coat chicken thoroughly. Add coconut milk.

Simmer gently for 15-20 minutes or until chicken is cooked through.

Meanwhile cook rice.

Place rice in pan with $1\frac{1}{4}$ to $1\frac{1}{2}$ times water to rice.

Bring to boil. Cook for 10 minutes only from moment rice comes to boil. Fluff up with fork.

To serve, pile rice into bowl. Spoon chicken over rice. Sprinkle with lots of freshly-chopped coriander and flaked roasted almonds.

Note: You can of course use ordinary rice – but Thai jasmine rice has a lovely, delicate, fragrant aroma.

oriental duck stir–fry
with noodles

Ingredients
(Serves 4)

4 duck breasts

oil for cooking

1 onion sliced

1 red pepper, cored and sliced

1 yellow pepper, cored and sliced

3 pinches chilli powder

250g (9oz) leaf spinach (baby)

noodles

salt and pepper

chives for garnish

For the sauce:

2 garlic cloves, crushed

juice of 1 lemon

4 tbsp runny honey

3 tbsp dark soy sauce

Method

Score duck skin with sharp knife.

Heat oil in griddle pan or large frying pan.

Seal duck on both sides, then cook for 5-6 minutes each side or longer, depending on taste.

Meanwhile, in separate pan, stir-fry onion, until softened, then peppers.

Sprinkle in chilli powder, stir and allow to cook.

When duck is cooked, put on one side to keep warm.

Pour off any excess oil but leave meat juices in pan. Return to heat.

Add garlic, honey, soy sauce and squeeze of lemon. Allow to cook.

When stir-fry is almost ready, add spinach and cook for about a minute, until just wilted. Season with salt and pepper and toss.

Meanwhile carve duck into slices.

To serve, pile stir-fry onto a platter. Arrange duck slices on top. Then drizzle over honey and soy sauce mixture.

Serve with noodles.

chicken, ham and leek pie

Ingredients
(Serves 6)

450-700g (1-1½ lb) cooked chicken or turkey

225g (8oz) cooked ham

2 leeks, trimmed

350g (12oz) Mascarpone or cream cheese

1 egg, beaten

1 tsp wholegrain mustard

1 tsp English mustard

oil for cooking

butter for cooking

salt and pepper

225g (8oz) ready-made puff pastry

1 beaten egg, to glaze

Method
Pre heat oven to 200°C/400°F/gas mark 6.

Melt butter and oil in large frying pan.

Slice leeks into 2.5cm (1-inch) lengths, add to pan and sweat until softened.

Take off heat and keep warm. Cut chicken and ham into bite-sized pieces and place, along with leeks, in bottom of 1.4 litre (2½ pint) pie dish.

In bowl combine Mascarpone cheese, egg and two mustards. Season with salt and pepper and mix together thoroughly all ingredients. Spoon mixture into pie dish.

Roll out pastry into oval about 5cm (2-inch) larger than top of pie dish. Cut off narrow strip from edge of pastry and press onto rim of dish. Brush rim with egg glaze.

Lay rest of pastry over top of pie dish. Trim and flute edges, then brush with egg glaze. Using small sharp knife, make few incisions in centre of pastry to allow steam to escape when baked.

Place pie on baking sheet, then bake in oven for about 30 minutes – or until pastry is well risen and browned.

caramelised pork chops
with onion confit

Ingredients
(Serves 4)

4 pork chops

salt and pepper

2 tsp granulated golden sugar

1 tbsp olive oil

2 tbsp balsamic vinegar

2 tbsp tomato ketchup

4 tbsp water

1 tbsp olive oil

3 large onions, peeled and sliced

1 tbsp golden granulated sugar

225g (8oz) tagliatelle – fresh or dried

Method
First make onion confit.

Heat oil in pan, add sliced onions and cook gently until softened.

Add sugar, continue to heat gently, stirring frequently until onions are reduced and golden brown – up to half an hour.

Meanwhile pre-heat oven to 200°C/400°F/gas mark 6.

Season pork chops and sprinkle with sugar on both sides.

Heat oil in large frying pan and cook chops for about 5 minutes, turning frequently until well browned.

Transfer chops and cooking juices to ovenware casserole dish and bake for 12-15 minutes.

Cook tagliatelle, following manufacturer's instructions on packet.

Remove casserole dish from oven and return to high heat on hob. Remove chops and keep warm.

Add to pan balsamic vinegar, tomato ketchup and water. Allow the sauce to reduce, stirring well.

Sauce is now ready to serve.

Drain pasta, and serve with chops, sauce and onion confit.

sausage and lentil supper

Ingredients
(Serves 4)

450g (1lb) good quality sausages

1 large onion, sliced

4 leeks, cleaned, trimmed and sliced

2 garlic cloves, crushed

110g (4oz) pre-cooked green lentils (optional)

110g (4oz) dry red lentils – from packet

50g (2oz) butter

oil

110g (4oz) smoked bacon, cut into lardon strips

175ml (6fl oz) vegetable stock

1 large jar Passata (thick sieved tomatoes)

parsley to garnish

Method
Half-cook sausages in large frying pan. Brown on all sides.

In separate pan melt oil and butter. Add onions and soften, then garlic and leeks.

Cook gently for few minutes then add bacon.

Cook for 5 more minutes then add red lentils, Passata and vegetable stock.

Add sausages, put lid on top and simmer gently on hob for 20-25 minutes.

Just before serving add green lentils (if using), stir well and warm through.

Finish off with touch of olive oil and plenty of parsley.

steak au poivre

Ingredients
(Serves 4)

4 x 125g (4½oz) fillet steaks

2 tbsp green peppercorns (in brine)

25g (1oz) butter

oil for cooking

75ml (3fl oz) brandy

75ml (3fl oz) white wine

150ml (¼ pint) beef stock

75ml (3fl oz) double cream

50g (2oz) butter, diced

For the lemon dressing:
4 tbsp olive oil

juice of 2 lemons

salt and pepper

Method
Strain peppercorns and wash.

Coat one side of steaks with peppercorns and season with salt.

Melt butter and oil in large frying pan.

Cook steaks on both sides until medium-rare (or to taste).

Remove from pan and keep warm.

Pour off any excess oil but leave meat residue in pan. Add brandy to pan and flame.

Add wine and reduce until syrupy.

Add stock and bring to the boil. Add cream and diced butter.

Stir and season to taste.

Strain sauce over steaks.

Serve with 125g (5oz) French beans, tossed in well-blended lemon dressing.

crêpes suzette

Ingredients

(Serves 4)

For the pancakes:

110g (4oz) plain flour

pinch of salt

1 egg, beaten

300ml (½ pint) milk

1 tbsp oil plus more for frying

For the orange and Grand Marnier sauce:

50g (2oz) unsalted butter

50g (2oz) caster sugar

grated rind and juice of 2 large oranges

grated rind and juice of one large lemon

4 tbsp brandy or Grand Marnier

icing sugar (optional)

Pancake Method

Sift flour and salt into bowl and make 'well' in centre.

Add egg and gradually add half milk, stirring constantly. Add oil and beat well until smooth.

Add remaining milk and leave to stand for 30 minutes.

Heat 15cm (6-inch) omelette pan and add few drops of oil.

Pour in tablespoon of batter and tilt pan to coat bottom evenly. Cook until the underside is brown.

Turn over and cook underside for about 10 seconds.

Turn out onto tea towel and cover.

Continue to make pancakes with remaining batter.

Orange Sauce Method

Melt butter in frying pan.

Add sugar, orange rind and juice, lemon rind and juice and heat until sauce is bubbling.

Add the brandy or Grand Marnier and continue heating until sauce has reduced to 'jammy' consistency.

Fold each pancake into quarters, and place in sauce. Coat well, and turn once or twice until pancakes are heated through.

Turn out onto serving dish, dust with icing sugar and eat while hot.

warm berry trifle

Ingredients

(Serves 6)

6 trifle sponges

3 eggs and 3 yolks

25g (1oz) caster sugar

300ml (½ pint) milk

300ml (½ pint) double cream

2 tbsp liqueur (Grand Marnier or brandy)

350g (12oz) pack frozen mixed Summer fruit berries

vanilla extract/vanilla pod

For the meringue topping:

3 egg whites

175g (6oz) soft brown sugar

toasted almond flakes

Method

Preheat oven to 180°C/350°F/gas mark 4.

Butter 2 pint baking dish.

Slice sponges.

Place fruit in base of pie dish. Arrange sponges on top and sprinkle with liqueur.

In another bowl mix together eggs, egg yolks and sugar.

Add milk, cream and vanilla extract (or seeds from vanilla pod) and whisk well. Pour this custard over sponges and leave to soak for ten minutes.

Place dish in roasting tin or bain marie filled with enough water to come half-way up baking dish. Place in oven and bake for 40-45 minutes until custard is set.

In clean bowl, whisk egg whites until stiff. Add half sugar and beat again until glossy and peaks return. Fold in rest of the sugar.

Spoon this meringue mix over pudding. Sprinkle with almonds and return to oven for another 5-10 minutes or until meringue has browned.

Serve hot from oven.

INDEX

TASTE IS CENTRAL to everything we produce at Wilkin & Sons which is why we're pleased to be sponsors of '*OUT TO LUNCH WITH BRIAN TURNER*'.

Everyone knows that good food is all about taste – yet that's not what actually tempts us to try things.

TO ATTRACT, FOOD HAS TO LOOK GOOD – whether it is a beautifully presented meal or a simple piece of fruit. But for us to really enjoy it and return again, it also needs to taste good. It's a paradox then, that while farmers have been under increasing pressure to produce food that looks good, it is flavour that has suffered.

At Wilkin & Sons we've not followed this trend. We cannot. Our jams, jellies and marmalades stand on their taste alone. Every piece of fruit we grow or buy has to deliver the finest taste irrespective of looks. Take the strawberry for example.

We've been growing our own strawberries at Tiptree since before Queen Victoria's coronation. Yet we've never been moved to change to newer, more prolific varieties. As Peter Wilkin explains: "Tiptree Strawberry Jam tastes much the same today as it would have done one hundred years ago. We're not against change, we simply haven't found anything that tastes better."

As the world becomes more accessible and more obsessed with convenience, many old varieties of fruit, with their distinctive flavours, are lost along the way. Who remembers the medlar for example? Much loved during the Victorian period, it has been grown in this country for over four hundred years and does, actually, make a lovely jelly!

BUT THERE IS GOOD NEWS! Because of our refusal to compromise, you can still experience the old flavours, as you can the new, by simply spreading jam on a slice of bread or toast. You could even use a spoonful in your own cooking. It takes no time and the results can be stunning.

TRY THIS TEST. Among our jams made from the traditional fruit we've grown ourselves are Quince, Medlar, Loganberry, Damson and Greengage – why not try them in your favourite recipes? Add Medlar Jelly to your gravy, melt Loganberry Conserve over ice cream, make a quince upside-down pudding. Or use Damson or Greengage Conserves in your tarts and cakes. Use your imagination and let any one of the 80 different Tiptree products help make the simplest of meals something special.

TIPTREE IS AND ALWAYS WILL BE – *ALL ABOUT TASTE.*